GROWING THROUGH DIVORCE

Rev. James J. Young, C.S.P.

PAULIST PRESS
New York, N.Y. / Ramsey, N.J.

Photo Credits
Cover Photos: Jean Claude Le Jeune, John Glaser
Thomas Ackerson: 14
Craig Callan: 22; 50
Ellen Kenny: 4
Mia et Klaus: 32; 42
Rick Smolan: iv

Designer: Emil Antonucci

Nihil Obstat
Msgr. Carroll E. Satterfield
Censor Librorum

Imprimatur
Most Rev. William D. Borders, D.D.
Archbishop of Baltimore
October 31, 1979

Library of Congress
Catalog Card Number: 79-90993

ISBN: 0-8091-2267-7

Published by Paulist Press
Editorial Office: 1865 Broadway, New York, N.Y. 10023
Business Office: 545 Island Road, Ramsey, N.J. 07446

Printed and bound in the
United States of America

CONTENTS

1. Background
2. Why So Much Divorce in American Society?
3. Building a New Life After Separation and Divorce
4. What Did Jesus Say About Divorce and Remarriage?
5. The Effect of Divorce on Children
6. The Parish and the Divorced Catholic
7. Starting a Parish-Divorced Catholics Group

BACKGROUND

The purpose of this program is to make American Catholics more understanding of the complex phenomenon of widespread divorce among committed Christians. It will explore the causes of divorce, as well as the painful adjustment faced by those who divorce and their children. It will focus on the religious and spiritual dimensions of this personal crisis and describe some concrete paths for healing and reconciliation to and for the Church community.

Because the complex social conditions which contribute to so much divorce in our contemporary society are not well known, there is often an unfortunate tendency to blame the divorced entirely for their difficulties. We will look at some of the powerful social forces which are reshaping the institution of marriage as we have known it and contributed to the problem so many Americans are having in attempting to build the lasting marriages they want.

We are beginning to get a clearer picture of the impact of divorce, and gaining a better hold on the shape of the transition every divorced person must make. We will follow the divorce recovery process with some men and women who could be your neighbors. Divorce is always hard on children, and it is hard on them in many different ways depending on the way the parents handle the divorce. We will explore the stress children experience and helpful ways to guide them through this perilous adjustment.

Divorce is a profound human crisis for everyone who divorces, raising troubling questions about personal values and the meaning of life. For the committed Christian the crisis is sharpened by traditional Christian values about marriage permanence and the failure which divorce represents. Divorce brings heavy doses of guilt and loss to the Catholic. We will look at the basic Christian teachings and values around marriage, divorce and remarriage, and look at the many ways in which the Church is attempting today to help the divorced person. The whole religious discussion will be brought home to the parishes where people live, and practical strategies for neighbor helping neighbor will be described.

Confronting divorce in contemporary society may seem like an overwhelming task at times, but this book is designed to give the concerned Christian some practical handles for understanding the issues and reaching out to those who are suffering.

WHY SO MUCH DIVORCE IN AMERICAN SOCIETY?

When Bill Martin got married in 1955, he never thought his marriage would fail. Bill pledged "for better, for worse; for richer, for poorer; in sickness and in health; until death do us part." Yet today Bill and his former wife have parted.

Widespread divorce among American Catholics is a phenomenon of the last decade, and is especially puzzling because Bill Martin and the other Catholic college graduates of that postwar era had many of the best advantages American society could offer—fine education, economic opportunity, and social mobility. They married soon after college, began to raise big families, and advanced quickly in business and the professions. They were serious, observant Catholics who built hundreds of new suburban parishes and parochial schools. Many of their classmates became priests and sisters in record numbers.

Then slowly the American divorce rate began to rise. By the mid-60s it became clear that American Catholics were, for the first time in history, providing their full share of broken American marriages. How could this have happened? Some said it was because American Catholics had become too "Americanized." A growing secularization was promoting disaffection from patterns of Church life and from traditional Catholic values about permanent marriage.

Others said that the enormous draining demands of the corporate structure, mobility and the loss of family ties and supports, and the pace of modern living, all were tearing the fragile marital relationship apart. On the other hand, it was argued that positive new values learned from both Church and society, values about greater intimacy and friendship in marriage and personal development, were causing a "crisis of rising expectations" in marriage which bred pervasive marital dissatisfaction. Whatever may have been the complex reasons, by the early 1970s divorce among American Catholics had become the major pastoral problem facing the American Church.

Steve McBride returned from two tours of duty as a combat Marine in Viet Nam, and married Cindy, his high school sweetheart. It was a festive wedding, and everyone toasted the beautiful couple, wishing them a long and happy life.

Two and a half years later, Cindy sued Steve for divorce. Several times ordinary adjustment squabbles erupted into violent quarrels, in which Steve lost control and beat her. The third time Cindy was hospitalized with a broken nose and a cracked rib. Steve couldn't explain how it happened. A recent report from the Veterans Administration calculates that one out of five combat veterans from the Viet Nam War are emotionally disabled, and their lives have been scarred by chronic unemployment, drug abuse and marital breakdown. Past wars have always had a disruptive effect on marriage with shell-shocked veterans unable to maintain stable unions, but no war seems to have taken more of a toll on its fighting men than Viet Nam. The unpopularity of the war at home; the intense, bloody combat; and the widespread presence of alcohol and drugs left many young men permanently wounded.

When Jack and Patty Novack married, Jack was working as a counterman at McDonald's and Patty was a clerk-typist at a bank. Patty soon became pregnant, and when she had to leave work in her eighth month, things became financially tight for them. Jack kept hoping to get into the autoworkers' union and even tried sales on the side, but nothing worked out. Patty had a hard time with the baby, but once she was back on her feet, she began waitressing at nights to help out financially. They began to see less and less of each other. When Patty got pregnant again within several months, they were really depressed. They couldn't believe it, and they even considered an abortion; but they couldn't do it. Their second baby was born ten months later. They borrowed money from parents, but hated doing it. They seemed to be always behind, fighting over money, diapers, bills; they always seemed tired and on edge. One day Patty blew up, told Jack the whole marriage had been a mistake, and left; she said she couldn't take it anymore, and that she wanted a divorce.

There are stories and more stories of young Americans who married, fully expecting their marriage would last, who are now divorced. They ask themselves over and over again, "Why?" "What went wrong?" "Why couldn't we make it?" "We had everything going for us, why didn't it work?" Researchers continually look at these stories attempting to piece together the clues to find answers to these complicated questions. If most Americans think back to their childhoods, they find they knew very few people who were divorced. If people did divorce in the 40's or 50's, they certainly kept it a secret or moved away. It wasn't talked about; it didn't happen to the good families.

Ordinary Americans helped by more scientific research have begun to puzzle through the high divorce rates and are coming to some sharp conclusions about why so much divorce:

1. Industrialization has made us a nation of gypsies with over half the American population living more than a thousand miles from their birthplaces. Modern economic life demands men and women who will relocate if a job demands it, and will adapt their day to the hours a plant operates. Gone is the settled life in a small town where father walked to work, and mother was at home raising children. This mobile work force gains the advantages and comfort affluence brings, but often sacrifices much in kinship support and cultural bonds. A consumer society encourages appetites for possessions and convenience which leaves many married couples straining to keep up. Economic pressures, such as debilitating inflation and chronic joblessness, all burden the fragile marriage relationship.

2. Divorce has become more acceptable, and has become the ordi-

nary solution to an intolerable marriage in every corner of American society. Just twenty-five years ago anthropoligist Margaret Mead commented on the image of the divorced person as selfish, irresponsible, or shady. But now legal barriers to divorce have fallen after a decade of rewriting divorce laws in the United States, making divorce cheaper, quicker and easier to obtain. Job discrimination against the divorced has lessened. In the American Catholic community, almost every family now has some near relative who is divorced. People still consider divorce unfortunate, but also have begun to accept that when it touches their loved ones, it may have been inevitable. Fewer Americans are willing to stick out an unsatisfactory marriage. The social and religious prohibitions have evaporated so quickly, that some social commentators believe today we have lost a kind of necessary social glue which helped people work through problems and think twice about ending a marriage. At times today, there seems to be an unfortunate pressure to separate quickly and find someone new before it's too late.

3. The changing status of women in our society and all those factors we gather under the heading of the "women's movement" have brought women the freedom to divorce. At one time, the great majority of married women were financially dependent on their husbands. Today more and more women have personal earning power and job skills, and for the first time in American history can now choose to end a marriage and be confident that they can make it on their own. In recent decades the changing American marketplace has created an enormous number of new jobs for women.

4. Some observers feel we are gripped by a crisis of "rising expectations in marriage." Never before have so many people looked for so much from their marriages, and never before have they been so likely to be dissatisfied. We Americans seem to cherish our right to the unimpeded pursuit of happiness, no matter how much pain that pursuit may bring. We don't like to be fenced in, and we seem to worship personal freedom. We feel that all persons should be allowed to move if they don't like their present homes, change schools, change friends, change political parties, change religious affiliations, change partners. It is argued that, if past mistakes can be repaired in every other field of human relations, why should marriage be the exception? Our movies and television and novels and songs condition

us to want personal fulfillment, personal growth, intimacy, friendship, happiness, and on and on. As good as all these things are, they can all together become a heady wine and an irresistible pull away from struggling to make a relationship work. Some say that we Americans have not yet learned how to build the kind of marriage relationships we want. The new kind of marriage taking shape in our culture demands much more on an interpersonal level of its partners than marriages did in the past; yet we do not seem to have developed the necessary skills at communication, expressing and receiving feelings, supporting each other's personal growth, building friendships outside the marriage—which long-term modern marriage demands.

5. *New York* magazine recently published an autobiographical account by a writer-editor who had left a good job and an unsatisfactory marriage to fulfill his long-standing fantasy of living on a South Sea island. It was by no means clear that he was glad he had done so; or that things had worked out well. Yet his abandonment of responsibility in a quest for self-fulfillment was published, presumably, to interest readers who had their own comparable fantasies.

In another magazine a woman told of leaving her comfortable marriage to realize her life-long amition to become a writer. She was quite sure she was right to have done so, despite the insecurity and recurrent unhappiness of her new life. Although it is unusual for someone to leave a marriage solely to achieve self-realization, it does happen occasionally. Robert Weiss, a sociologist who studies marriage, calls this sense of obligation to pursue one's own goals at the expense of marriage the *ethic of self-realization.* Today even when the pursuit of self-realization does not produce marital separation, it does seem to contribute a great deal of marital strife. One spouse may feel it is improper to interfere with the other spouse's freedom to grow, even though the spouse's new freedom contributes to the breakdown of the marriage. Or one finds another spouse who is guilty over the breakdown of a marriage, convinced that he didn't enable his wife to grow. Never before have so many married people been tormented by the question, "Have I made a mistake?" So many dream continually of meeting some new person who will bring them the happiness and fulfillment for which they yearn. This may be one of the most significant factors contributing to our escalating divorce rate. The genie has gotten out of the jar, and we can't get the lid back on.

6. Lastly, there is no question that the relaxation of religious stigma associated with divorce has contributed to the freedom to divorce. We have no evidence that shifting attitudes in the Catholic community contribute to more divorce, or that one's Catholic faith acts any longer as a serious deterrent to ending an unsatisfactory marriage. There is some evidence that Catholics divorce slightly less than the population at large, and there is evidence that people who are religiously observant divorce less than the population as a whole. This means that devout Jews, Protestants and Catholics divorce less than people who do not practice any religion at all. It seems that those who accept traditional religious values against divorce invest more in working out the crises that come to marriage, and may have more support available to them in their congregations. One thing is certain, the current amount of divorce among Catholics testifies to the fact that Catholics have become as American as apple pie. The unique supports that the Catholic community provided its members in the past have mostly evaporated and Catholics are as affected by cultural forces in our society as anyone else.

How much divorce is there? Arriving at reliable estimates of the rate of marital separation in the United States is no easy task. Statistics on divorce are available from the U.S. Census Bureau, yet they don't tell the whole story about marriages in trouble. Not every separation ends in divorce; many, perhaps most, end in reconciliation, although many of these reconciliations will later give way to new separations. Almost certainly no more than half of all separations end in divorce. The divorce rate in this country has increased steadily since before the turn of the century, with the exception of a period of near stability in the 1920's. There was a sharp rise during the years of World War II, followed by a drop to a much lower level and another time of near stability during most of the 1950's. The steady increase in the rate resumed in 1962, picked up speed by 1965, and by 1971 had moved beyond the peak year of 1946. In 1975 for the first time in American history a million marriages ended in divorce, and that rate continues today. It is said that of all couples entering first marriages this year, we can anticipate, if current trends continue, that 35% of those marriages will eventually end in divorce. If these trends continue for several more years, we may soon be able to say that an American marriage is more likely to end in divorce than not.

If a couple lives in a neighborhood where they may know about fifty other couples through the Church, schools, or community activities, they will know an average of only one or two who separate in any given year. As time goes on, of course, many more of the couples in their friendship circle will separate.

There is certainly an element of social gain in the fact that men and women who make mistakes in choosing a partner or find themselves in a marriage which is hopeless and destructive to them and their children are able to divorce. Yet we are also tormented by doubts about what is wrong in a society whose present values and institutional arrangements encourage so much disruption in marriage relationships and so much long-term suffering.

Morton Hunt draws the following generalization from a detailed, national study he conducted about divorce in the United States:

1. Today the time between separation and civil divorce is less than one year, whereas it was two years in 1960.

2. Divorced men remarry sooner and in greater numbers than women, so that more unremarried women than men accumulate in the population. In 1976 there were three divorced women for every two divorced men in the population.

3. Half of all divorces are granted within the first seven years of marriage. The highest rate of divorce takes place during the second year of marriage, but less than a tenth of divorces take place in that year. People continue to divorce in every year of married life; over a third of all divorces occur after ten or more years, over a tenth after twenty or more.

4. The median age of men at the time of divorce is a little under 33, of women, 30. The median age at separation is one year less than divorce. There is no divorce boom in middle age today; there are more divorces at mid-life today only because there are more divorces at every stage of life.

5. The older people are when they divorce, the longer it takes them to remarry and the less chance there is that they will ever do so.

6. The chance that you are currently divorced, if you are black, is about a third higher than if you are white; the chance that you are currently separated, if you are black, is nearly six times as great as if you are white.

7. The lower in the socio-economic scale you are, the greater your chance of divorce if you are a man or a non-working wife. Many people think that divorce is most common among the relatively affluent, sophisticated, or discontented people of our society; the families of working-class people are supposed to be rock-solid. The truth is just the reverse, and has long been so. For the past fifty years, unskilled or semi-skilled laborers have been about three times as likely to get divorced as professional or business people. The rising divorce rate can be accounted for by what one observer has called the "democratization of divorce"; it is now touching almost all groups in the society equally.

8. The typical divorced person is more likely to be a parent than not. In 1973 close to 60% of all divorcing people had children under 18. There continues to be evidence that people do work harder at keeping a marriage together for the sake of children.

Answering the question—why so much divorce in American society?—is most difficult and challenging. The best researchers confess the limited nature of their findings and plead for more social investments in trying to find out why. Religious leaders, politicians, educators, trade-unionists—all who care about the quality of our society voice alarm about the continuing high rates of marital disruption in our country. But most of all these statistics involve men and women, our neighbors, who are in pain and in need of help. Stabilizing marriage and helping contemporaries find the happiness they seek is one of the most crucial issues facing us.

References:

Hunt, Morton and Hunt, Bernice. *The Divorce Experience.* New York: McGraw-Hill, 1977.

Weiss, Robert S. *Marital Separation.* New York: Basic Books, 1975.

BUILDING A NEW LIFE AFTER SEPARATION AND DIVORCE

No one is ever ready for a divorce. Everyone expected his or her marriage to work at the start. For almost every divorced person, divorce comes as a rude shock. "I never thought it would happen to me!" "I always thought we would live happily ever after—this just wasn't supposed to happen!" "I should have seen it coming, but I didn't. I just blocked it out. I couldn't face the fact that the marriage wasn't working!"

Most friends and relatives of someone who divorces want to reach out and help, but they often don't know what to do. They don't want to pry into all the intimate details of the failed relationship, and they don't want to take sides. Yet we are learning that there are some very concrete, practical things friends and loved ones can do that can make a significant difference for the divorcing person. In order to know how to help, it's important, first of all, to understand better what happens to people when they get divorced. What is the shock like? How long does it take to get over it? What are the special problems and fears of the divorced person?

Here are some of the key issues faced by the divorcing person:

1. The Emotional Impact of Separation

Almost all divorced persons feel deeply sad after their partner leaves, even though they may not want a reconciliation. They feel a deep sense of loss; and often are surprised to find that they miss the other person. One man couldn't wait to leave his wife, with whom he had had much tension over a long period of time, but once he left he couldn't get her off his mind. He would daydream about her and become very restless, and then get angry at himself for thinking about her. He found the only thing that made him feel better was to get in his car and drive by her house.

Divorce brings with it a loss of attachment. Even in marriages that were not successful, two people may have become very attached to each other and become dependent on each other in many ordinary ways. Even though one no longer loves the other or trusts the other, he may find himself missing the other. Sometimes, at this low point, one may begin to feel abandoned by the other and blame the other for one's present distress. "If only she had been different, this wouldn't have happened and I wouldn't feel so bad."

The divorcing person often experiences an aching loneliness; this loneliness is all the harder to bear because one doesn't know exactly whom one misses. It's a loneliness that seems impossible to fill, because there is no new person in one's life. These first stages of divorce are often accompanied by tension, vigilance, restlessness and sleeplessness. The divorcing person is frequently tormented with guilt, blame, and a sense of failure. If one has been left by the other, there can be a tendency to identify with the rejecting other in viewing oneself as unlovable and unattractive. One can feel like the bad sheep in one's family, a shame to one's neighbors and friends, a disreputable and fallen person.

Sometimes the person who is separated gets drawn into an obsessional review of the marriage, playing over in one's mind all the ups and downs of the marriage. One finds one's life turned inside out: there are new tasks to meet, a practical reorganization of one's life is demanded; children must be handled alone, there is less money; in one word, the divorcing person experiences "overload."

Yet one can also experience dramatic mood swings; one feels in the dumps one day, and on top of the world the next day. There is some sense of loss, yet some sense of gain. Things are harder being alone, yet they are better because one is free of the spouse who caused so much upset and pain. On the high days one is ready to build a whole new life, but several days later one may feel unable to cope with grocery shopping. The recently divorced have been shown to be accident-prone, distracted, impulsive, given to nervous laughter and easy tears. It's a very difficult time.

Yet as stressful as this adjustment may be for the normal person, one does gradually begin to feel better. With the passage of time, one begins to pile up some small successes, maximizes one's gains, and feels less frightened about the future.

2. The Continuing Relationship with the Former Spouse

Even though two persons decide that they can no longer live together as husband and wife, they will be enormously fortunate if they can discover how to be friends. This is especially important if they must continue to cooperate around the raising of children. Many couples have found it helpful to structure their continuing contact, thinking through relationships with family and friends and agreeing on public versions of their marital problems. As much as people may try to be civil, there is always continuing anger, especially as the difficulties brought on by the divorce pile up. There are always disagreements over money, possessions, and children. Sometimes the process of legal divorce aggravates a delicate relationship. This anger often spills over into a feeling of betrayal accompanied by lingering hostility, especially if one spouse left for another person. Maintaining friendly ties and a cooperative spirit can make an enormous difference in the long run.

3. The Impact of Separation on Relations with Kin, Friends, and Others

The relatives of a divorcing couple find themselves torn apart by conflicting loyalties, and their parents can be tormented by a deep sense of disappointment. One may have been the star athlete or scholarship winner in a family, the apple of one's parents eyes as a youth, but now one feels that one's standing is diminished and one has brought shame on the family. Parents often torture themselves with self-doubt: "What did we do wrong?" The divorcing woman may feel dependent on her parents or brothers and sisters at this difficult adjustment time, yet in conflict because she does not want to lose her autonomy. Men say that they are often made to feel that as the stronger sex they should have been able to hold things together and "keep her happy."

Men sometimes experience a keen loss of face on the job, sometimes feeling that their future promotions may be jeopardized by this appearance of instability. A man usually is deeply unsettled by leaving his home, and living in a rented room with friends, or living back at his parents' home. Men tend to lose touch with their in-laws, but women sometimes do not because they have custody of the children. Married friends tend to rally around at first, often reaching out to the individual spouses, but friendships tend to gradually fade as the divorced persons begin to establish a new identity and a new network of friends. The divorcing person often feels isolated, feels she doesn't quite fit in any more, nervous about relating to former friends and associates, yet still in search of good, new friends.

4. The Impact of Separation on Children and the Parents' Relationships with Them

More will be said later on the adjustment children face after their parents separate. Briefly, divorce is always hard on children. Some children seem to regress or stagnate for a while, yet there is indication that some children are challenged to mature sooner and come to grips with the adjustment very well. It appears from research that the most important determinant of the well-being of the children in a one-parent family is the mother's ability to cope with the challenges she faces. (93% of American children from families where there is divorce live with their mothers.) In this transitional early phase, the mother becomes a key coping model for the children. If the mother manages the adjustment fairly well, usually the children will respond accordingly. The custodial parent in this new family situation must learn how to manage responsibility for discipline alone, and take one's own counsel in many confusing situations where there is no one else available to consult. Since the father is usually no longer a member of the child's household, his household roles disappear, demanding that he build a new relationship with the child.

5. New Friendships and Dating

Loneliness and loss of self-esteem make new relationships especially important for the divorcing person. A new friend of the opposite sex can reassure one of worth and attractiveness and also help relieve loneliness. A night out may be a welcome relief from the overload situation at home. New friends can also help one talk through and integrate the mountain of new experience and adjustments one is facing. There is a danger of hasty sexual involvement at this time as a way of proving one's self worth and attractiveness, but in these early stages when one is still working through the loss of the former relationship, these liaisons can be very problematic. Sexual activity at this time may lead one to feel exploited or used, or feel that one is moving rapidly into a new commitment one can't handle. Support groups at this time can be a very important cushion for the person going through the adjustment, protecting him or her from hasty over-involvements in new relationships.

Again and again, people ask, "When will it all be over? When will I feel like myself again?" Even though people come to a divorce from many different places—marriages of various lengths, different numbers of children, varied economic levels, wide-ranging amounts of pain and hostility endured within the marriage—yet we know that divorce is always traumatic. Even though we are getting more used to divorce in this society, and even though we all know more people who are divorced, there is no indication that divorce is getting any easier in American society. It shakes everyone to the roots. It raises profound questions about personal worth, personal goals, and the very meaning of life. For all the variations one finds in divorced persons and for all the different stories they tell about the varied details of their failed marriages, adjustment to a divorce takes almost everyone several years.

The process of dealing with guilt and loss, a radically altered life style, the collapse of a social system and the need to establish a new network of friends and support—this process will be somewhat different for every person, yet for almost everyone it takes two to four years. Professionals who help people with divorce adjustment always counsel them to give themselves time. They are told to beware of a hasty sense of recovery—one may rapidly get some practical issues in hand, or one may experience some immediate ways in which one's life is better, and one may feel great very soon; but there are long-term, tough issues about one's identity, one's future and one's capacity to find happiness that require giving oneself time. Most researchers agree that it takes a good year just to separate out from all the feelings and pain of the failed marriage; one has to go through all the holidays and anniversaries and experience onself making it over the months to begin to get some distance. Even when one begins to feel successful in establishing a new single life, it takes another good year to begin to feel secure in one's new situation. There will be successes and failures to be balanced out, and one has to have some sense over a long time that the successes are becoming the majority.

It's hard to be a single person in American society. Divorced persons find a very strong tug back toward coupling. There is a continuing fantasy, "If only I could meet someone else—someone who would make me feel better—help me with all these problems—make me feel loved again." There's something very human about that fantasy, yet early on one is not ready to enter into a new relationship. One has a need to put together an autonomous personal existence, become one's own person. Divorce adjustment counselors all insist that the goal of divorce recovery work is not remarriage, but rather a new single life. For some divorced persons, this may be the first time in their lives that they have readily made it on their own, especially if they married young and never lived on their own.

Sustaining the personal growth and new single autonomy over a period of several years is very difficult, yet one finds a most attractive vitality in those who have shaped such a new single life. It's never without its problems, but one does feel proud of making it unmarried. This is where support groups or "Parents Without Partners" or an active parish community can all make an enormous difference for the divorced person.

Learning how to be friends with someone of the opposite sex, yet not moving quickly into a marriage relationship, is a kind of living which people have rarely seen in this day. People need companionship, especially companionship of the opposite sex, to help build a new self-image and reinforce personal growth. Yet these new relationships require a conscious openness about one's present situation, and the need to go slow. More and more divorced persons with the help of one another are learning how to build these new friendships.

The divorcing person needs allies during this difficult time, good friends who are available to them, whom they can cry with, or get angry with, or simply share everyday problems with. That ally may be an old friend, it may be someone one meets in a singles group or divorce group, or it may be a priest or pastoral minister. This ally needs to be patient with the divorcing person and be ready to stand by him or her through a difficult, tangled emotional transition that will take several years.

There is a great deal of information the divorcing person needs: information about one's new single status, raising children alone, taxes, the law, career opportunities, and on and on. Many of the new divorce groups and singles organizations provide some important lectures and workshops for the divorced person. Friends should encourage the separated person who is reluctant to venture forth to take advantage of these new opportunities. One's self esteem can be greatly enhanced by the company of others facing the same crisis who are seen to be making it.

The experts all seem to agree that a person who is ending a marriage needs to give him or herself two to four years to build a new life. It's important to have that consciousness from the start, so that one doesn't short circuit this necessary growth time. Some few people may move through this growth time more rapidly than others, and some may linger longer along the path to a new life. All the experts agree that taking oneself seriously at this time and being good to oneself takes time and hard work.

WHAT DID JESUS SAY ABOUT DIVORCE AND REMARRIAGE?

Christians are people who pattern their lives after the person and teaching of Jesus of Nazareth. For this reason, today more than ever, more and more devout Christians are reading and studying the Bible. When we were children we often learned phrases and pieces of the Scriptural portrait of Jesus, but all too often we missed the whole picture with all its shadings and brilliance. For example, when Catholics are asked what did Jesus say about divorce and remarriage, they are quick to respond "What God has joined together let no man put asunder" (Matthew 19:6). Unfortunately this phrase was often used to condemn the divorced and remarried. We are learning that there is much more to Jesus' words about divorce and remarriage, much more that can be of challenge and comfort to the divorced person.

To understand just what Jesus said about divorce and remarriage in the Scriptures, it's important that we know some of the background of the passages as they appear. We read in the Gospel of Mark:

Leaving there, Jesus came to the district of Judaea and the far side of the Jordan. And again the crowds gathered round him, and again he taught them, as his custom was. Some Pharisees approached him and asked, "Is it against the law for a man to divorce his wife?" They were testing him. He answered them, "What did Moses command you?" "Moses allowed us," they said, "to draw up a writ of dismissal and so to divorce." Then Jesus said to them, "It was because you were so unteachable that he wrote this commandment for you. But from the beginning of creation God made them male and female. This is why a man must leave his father and mother, and the two become one body. So then, what God has united, man must not divide." Back in the house the disciples questioned him again about this, and he said to them, "The man who divorces his wife and marries another is guilty of adultery against her. And if a woman divorces her husband and marries another she is guilty of adultery too" (Mark 10:1–12).

We read in the New Testament that the Pharisees were always trying to trap and embarrass Jesus. In one place they offer him a coin, and ask him if it is lawful to offer tribute to Caesar. You can almost see them smirking when you read the passage, figuring that anything Jesus says in answer to that question will get him into trouble.

Divorce and remarriage were permitted among the Jews in the time of Jesus. It is important to note that, in the time of Jesus, a man could divorce his wife, but a woman could not divorce her husband in Jewish law. Moses gave permission for a man to write a divorce notice and send his wife away. The rabbis or interpreters of the Law of Moses offered many different grounds that a man could cite in divorcing his wife.

There was one school of thought that held that a woman had to have left her husband and gone off with another man before he could divorce her. Another school of thought was much more lenient and held that a man could divorce his wife if he was generally unhappy with her, and even if she had turned out to be a poor wife and housekeeper. This was a fairly intense debate in the time of Jesus, and you can see how it was a perfect issue with which to try to trap Jesus.

How does Jesus answer them? Well, Jesus doesn't give them an answer, instead he asks them another question: "What did Moses command you?" When they give him the correct answer, Jesus then comments by moving the discussion to a different level. He appeals to a prior, more fundamental law, God's law of creation. "But from the beginning of creation, God made them male and female. This is why a man must leave his father and mother, and the two become one body." Jesus seems to be reminding them of something very important that they have forgotten in their whole discussion about the grounds of divorce. He seems to be saying, if you had things in proper perspective and if you understood what God intended from the beginning, you wouldn't be caught in all these arguments now. Jesus insists that marriage is of the very order of creation. God intended from the start that men and women be made for marriage—it's natural. "This is why a man must leave his father and mother, and the two become one body." They will become one not just because they want to become one; they will become one because that is the way they were made; the pull towards unity is in their very composition, in their hearts. "So then, what God has united, man must not divide." Man must not tear apart that union of husband and wife which is the very reality God intended.

Jesus seems to be saying you would not be arguing so lightly about divorce if you realized that marriage should be permanent and lasting, which is what God intended. Jesus is saying that permanence and fidelity in marriage is built into a man and a woman, and that divorce is a disfigurement of what God intended for men and women. So Jesus does not take sides in the divorce argument; he does not come out for strict or lenient grounds, rather he takes the occasion to tell his hearers that there should be no divorce. For divorce offends against the very way God made things. I think that we can say quite insistently that for Jesus in the New Testament there should be no divorce.

But that does not end the discussion of the sayings of Jesus on divorce. For when we read an account of the same scene and the same discussion in Matthew's Gospel we find a startling difference in the words of Jesus. The scene is almost verbatim what we read in Mark except for one very important line: "It was because you were so unteachable that Moses allowed you to divorce your wives, but it was not like this from the beginning.

Now this I say to you: the man who divorces his wife—*I am not speaking of unchastity*—and marries another, is guilty of adultery" (Matthew 19:8-9). The italicized words are not found in Mark's version, and when we read them in Matthew, it seems to say that a man can divorce his wife if she is unfaithful. This kind of unfaithfulness was the strict ground that the rabbis in the time of Jesus said was a ground of divorce. So whereas in Mark's account, Jesus grants no exception, in Matthew he seems to be willing to grant divorce if a woman has been unfaithful. How can this be so?

We know that the different gospels were written for different audiences. According to a tradition dating from the second century, St. Matthew wrote a gospel in the Jewish tongue. The Gospel of Matthew was probably written about forty years after the death of Jesus. The gospel was written not to tell the life of Jesus, but rather to report his sayings and deeds in such a way that they would convert, edify and bring men and women to believe. It is clear that Matthew was writing for Jewish Christians, and makes a special point of demonstrating by the use of many Old Testament quotations that the Jewish scriptures are fulfilled in the person and work of Jesus. The Gospels of Mark and Luke which probably were written for pagan audiences contain fewer indications that Jesus is the long expected one of Jewish history.

The Law of Moses on divorce is found in the 24th Chapter of the Book of Deuteronomy: "Supposing a man has taken a wife and consummated the marriage, but she has not pleased him and he has found some impropreiety of which to accuse her; so he has made out a writ of divorce for her and handed it to her and then dismissed her from his house . . ." (Deut. 24:1–4). This passage had many interpretations in the time of Jesus, and he refuses to give another interpretation; rather he points to a more fundamental law behind it, the law of God at creation. He argues that there should be no divorce at all, because God designed marriage to be permanent. Jesus appeals to a deeper truth. He is a true prophet, piercing to the heart of things, laying before his audience the pure demands of his Father, just as elsewhere in the Gospel he lays before them the radical demands of non-violence and poverty.

By the time Matthew's Gospel is put together about 40 years after the death of Jesus, the early Christian community has been struggling with living his teaching and struggling too with the problems of broken marriages in the world around them. It seems that in the community out of which Matthew's Gospel comes there were many Jews who became Christians as well as many pagans. It appears that some of these pagans had married within the degrees of kinship forbidden to a Jew; for example, pagan uncles may have married their nieces. This was an abomination to the Jews. So the Matthean community permitted divorce and remarriage in these controversial cases. The particular problem of marriage within the forbidden degrees of kinship may sound remote to us, but what is important for us is the principle by which they permitted such divorce and remarriage. They certainly know that Jesus had said there should be no divorce, but they saw themselves in a new situation where they had to legislate to this particular situation, i.e., they had to apply the overall teaching of Jesus to this difficult problem, so they permitted a limited amount of divorce and remarriage to redress this painful situation.

For us Christians it is the Gospel that is the norm of our lives, the whole Gospel as it has been passed on to us, not just the first level of the Gospel, the ministry of Jesus. The followers of Jesus obviously felt that they were bound by the Lord himself to apply his teaching to real life situations. Therefore in the Gospel we find the early Christian community preaching the call to permanence in marriage and proposing no divorce, but also permitting a limited amount of divorce and remarriage in certain extreme situations. This process of applying the teaching of Jesus to concrete situations and drawing out of men and women the best lives they were able to live was for them at the heart of being faithful to Jesus of Nazareth.

Matthew's Gospel is not the only place in the New Testament where we find the Church's sanctioning divorce and remarriage. The other significant place is in Saint Paul's First Letter to the Corinthians. The great apostle Paul, we know, carried the faith from the precincts of Palestine out into the pagan world. He founded many churches in the great cities of the ancient world, including Corinth. In Paul's day Corinth was a bustling city with a cosmopolitan population drawn from all parts of the Roman Empire. It was a center of government and of commerce; its population included Roman officials, military, businessmen, merchants and sailors from all over the empire. In a pagan world notoriously tolerant of sexual license, Corinth had a reputation for debauchery. The founding of the church in Corinth by Paul in early 51 A.D. is recorded in the Acts of the Apostles. Despite many difficulties and sufferings, when Paul departed from the city after eighteen months of apostolic activity he left behind a flourishing community of Jewish and Gentile converts.

In his first letter to the Corinthians, written about 57 A.D., Paul formulates answers to questions put to him in a letter from the Corinthian community, especially questions about marriage. In the seventh chapter of that letter, writing about marriage Paul says: "For the married I have something to say, and this is not from me but from the Lord, a wife must not leave her husband—or if she does leave him, she must either remain unmarried or else make it up with her husband—nor must a husband send his wife away." Paul clearly reiterates the ideal of the Lord. Then Paul goes on with more advice, this time stating clearly that he is speaking on his own: "The rest is from me and not from the Lord. If a brother has a wife who is an unbeliever, and she is content to live with him, he must not send her away; and if any woman has an unbeliever for her husband and he is content to live with her, she must not leave him. This is because the unbelieving husband is made one with the saints through his wife, and the unbelieving wife is made one with the saints through her husband. If this were not so, your children would be unclean, whereas in fact they are holy. However, if the unbelieving partner does not consent, they may separate; in these circumstances the brother or sister is not tied. God has called you to a life of peace" (1 Corinthians 7:10–11, 12–15).

What is startling about this passage is that Paul is sanctioning divorce. He says that if a marriage is broken down between two pagans after one of them becomes Christian, let it be so. Becoming a Christian in pagan Corinth would put a great strain on any marriage. Becoming a Christian meant that one had to separate onself from most of the public life of the city; one could not socialize in the usual ways or participate in the pagan public worship. It was a radical break from the whole society, much more serious than the conversion of one marriage partner in our own time. It's easy to understand how this would place a strain on a marriage. Apparently many such marriages must have been falling apart, and the Church in Corinth turned to Paul its founder for advice.

Paul has taught then the Lord's ideal for marriage as he repeats it in his letter. Yet Paul says even though the Lord insists upon the ideal of a permanent and lasting marriage, there are circumstances where such an ideal is not possible—such a circumstance being these struggled and strained Christian-pagan marriages. Paul then cites a higher principle: "For God has called you to a life of peace." So Paul repeats the ideal of the Lord and challenges his new Christian community to attempt to live up to it. But when he is faced with marriages that have irremediably broken down because of the conversion of one partner, he says let them part, "for God has called you to a life of peace."

So when we look at the New Testament evidence on divorce and remarriage we find Jesus' presenting a high ideal that marriage should be permanent and lifelong, because that is the way that God made men and women; he made them naturally to form a permanent union. But the early apostles recognize that the ideal is not always realized in the ordinary lives of men and women. Many conditions such as religious differences or long customs work against people realizing that ideal of permanent lasting love. So in those cases, Matthew and Paul permit divorce and remarriage for the greater good of the gospel and the greater good of the men and women involved.

Yet if we want to understand how Jesus related to divorced persons in his day, we should read the beautiful story in John's Gospel (John 4:4-42) about Jesus and the divorced woman he met at Jacob's well. Here we find the merciful Lord offering healing and new life to a woman who had been divorced five times.

We read that Jesus was travelling through Samaritan territory. The Jews considered Samaritans heretics and outcasts; they had once been part of the household of Israel but had in previous centuries intermarried with pagans and had separated themselves from the temple worship in Jerusalem. Jews had nothing to do with Samaritans for this reason. Jesus was, the Gospel tells us, a rabbi or teacher; he would have been recognizable as such by special dress. Further, rabbis never talked to women in public; it was said that if a rabbi met his mother on the street in Jerusalem, the rabbi would pass by her silently.

Imagine how startled the woman must have been when she came

to Jacob's well on her daily round and saw sitting there a Jewish rabbi. She may well have been afraid that he would chase her away, at least that he would ignore her. She is startled when he asks her for a drink. "What? You are a Jew, and you ask me, a Samaritan, for a drink?" Then Jesus says, "If you only knew what God is offering to you, and who it is that is saying to you, 'Give me a drink,' you would have been the one to ask, and he would have given you living water." Jesus is prepared to offer this woman the living water of his own person.

He then says to the puzzled woman, "Go and call your husband." The woman answers, "I have no husband." Jesus says, "You are right to say, 'I have no husband;' for although you have had five, and the one you have now is not your husband." The woman is startled that Jesus should know so much about her. "I see you are a prophet, sir . . . I know that Messiah—that is, Christ—is coming, and when he comes he will tell us everything." Jesus says, "I who am speaking to you, I am he."

What is dramatic about this story is that Jesus should choose to reveal himself to a woman who has been divorced five times. A scripture commentator once suggested that, if we are surprised to find Jesus revealing himself to a divorced woman, then we don't know Jesus very well. For if we read the Gospels in their entirety, we see that Jesus was always concerned about the outcasts, the rejected, the despised. There is a beautiful scene where Jesus is criticized for eating with tax collectors and sinners (Matthew 9:10–13); he answers his critics: "It is not the healthy who need the doctor, but the sick. Go and learn the meaning of the words: What I want is mercy, not sacrifice. And indeed I did not come to call the virtuous, but sinners." This quotation is not meant to imply that the divorced are sinners; in the time of Jesus those who suffered any kind of misfortune or disability in life were often considered sinners. The passage points out Jesus' concern for those who suffer.

We read further that the Samaritan woman then goes off into the town to announce the coming of Jesus. "Come and see a man who has told me everything I ever did; I wonder, if he is the Christ?" With that the people come pouring out to hear him, and soon many of them came to believe in him. It has been pointed out that this divorced woman of Samaria was one of the first apostles.

This story brings out very powerfully the fact that the same Lord who could preach such a demanding call to permanence in marriage could at the same time reach out with tenderness to this woman who had been divorced by five men. The strength and power of Jesus' teaching in no way separates him from the woman who has not been able to live up to it. How unlike the Lord we have so often been in the Christian community! How often in the past have we felt that our commitment to permanent marriage forced us to condemn and reject the divorced and remarried? Where Jesus offered this divorced woman a gesture of love and reconciliation—the living water of his own person—how often have we turned the divorced and remarried away from our Church?

The renewal of the Roman Catholic Church since the Second Vatican Council has been most of all a challenge directed to all of us to be more like Jesus Christ. The Roman Catholic Church is changing its attitudes towards the divorced and remarried because the Gospel of the Lord demands it. We are trying today in the Catholic community to be more like the Lord, doing all in our power to help Christians build the lasting marriages they want, while at the same time reaching out with care and support to our brothers and sisters who have been unable to achieve that beautiful goal. We are learning that there is no inconsistency involved in being against divorce but for divorced people.

In 1977 the American Catholic Bishops removed the penalty of automatic excommunication that had been attached to a second marriage by divorced Catholics. Speaking on behalf of his brother Bishops, Bishop Cletus O'Donnell of Madison, Wisconsin said, "The positive dimensions of this action are very real. It welcomes back to the community of believers in Christ all who may have been separated by excommunication. It offers them a share in all the public prayers of the church community. It restores their right to take part in church services. It removes certain canonical restrictions upon their participation in church life. It is a promise of help and support in the resolution of the burden of family life. Perhaps above all, it is a gesture of love and reconciliation from the other members of the Church."

THE EFFECT OF DIVORCE ON CHILDREN

Some years ago there was a common belief that if parents divorced, their children would grow up to be juvenile delinquents. About a decade ago, we Americans replaced that common belief with another one: for the children's sake, it is better to get a divorce. Most counsellors who help the children of divorce feel that the truth probably lies somewhere in the middle. Some children from divorced parents do turn out to be juvenile delinquents, while many others become responsible young citizens. Some children even improve and seem to do much better in their personal development after a turbulent marriage is ended by divorce; while there are other children who seem to thrive in a home where the parents have a very poor marriage. Understanding the effect of divorce on children is a very complex task.

One demographer estimates that in the 1970's between 20% and 30% of all American children under 18 have experienced the divorce of their parents; an additional 3 to 4% have been affected by an annulment or long-term separation. In 1970, about three-fifths of all the children of divorce were living with one remarried parent and a stepparent. There has been a 700% increase in the number of children affected by divorce in the United States since the turn of the century. This enormous amount of family disruption comes at a time of major questioning about raising children in our society. American parents seem uncertain about child-rearing, and report a loss of guidelines or supports for raising children. Today over half of American mothers work outside the home, a majority of them full-time. These mothers generally worry about whether they are providing adequate care for their children. These major societal problems are only aggravated by divorce. Divorce usually produces anger and a sense of failure for parents, issues of conflicting loyalty for children, and questions for everyone involved about whether the children will be harmed.

Dr. Robert Weiss, a research sociologist at the Laboratory for Community Psychiatry, Harvard Medical School, reports that the immediate response of most children of all ages to the news of parental separation is distress and anxiety. Children become tearful, tense and withdrawn. A minority of children, particularly among adolescents, seem able to take separation in stride. Some children may have written off one of the parents or become hostile towards him or her and are happy to see that parent depart. Most children indicate that they would like the parents to reconcile. Some try to bring the parents together themselves. Apart from the desire that their parents reconcile, most children's concerns focus on themselves. They are concerned about where they will live or with whom they will live. They want to know when they can see the departing parents. They worry about whether they will stay with their brothers and sisters. They want to know if the parent who has gone still cares for them.

The children of divorce are haunted by many real and imagined fears. Small children may voice a suspicion that they were responsible for the breakup. Older children may seem afraid about their future. They may think they will have to leave school and take a job, or fear that they will lose their friends now that their parents have separated.

Ordinarily the children accept the parents' decision regarding with whom they will live. Most children want to avoid deciding between the parents; they do not want to alienate either by choosing the other. The children know that these two people will always be their parents, even though the parents can no longer live with each other. For many children the anxiety produced by news of the separation seems to subside rather quickly. This is usually related to the custodial parent's capacity to manage his or her new situation and maintain the stable routines of ordinary life. Many parents report that their children adapted better to the changed living circumstances than they did.

Some children do display a wide variety of distress, ranging from disturbing emotional symptoms, such as nightmares, tantrums or severe withdrawal, to such less serious things as nail biting or occasional anger at one or both parents. Many custodial mothers report that their children become harder to handle after separation; some children refuse to see their father when he visits. In most cases such anger is short-lived, but it can continue indefinitely. Children cannot be forced to accept a divorce; they must accept it themselves and will adapt to it at their own speed. Dr. Richard Gardner, a child psychiatrist, says that children are far less fragile than most parents realize, and are much more capable of accepting the painful realities of life than is generally appreciated.

Judith S. Wallerstein and Joan B. Kelly, who have been studying the children of divorce in California since 1970, have found that most children, irrespective of age, are upset at first by parental separation. Somewhat more than half, however, return by the end of a year to normal development. At that time they appear essentially undamaged by the separation. They are likely still to remember its pain, and may regret that their parents decided on it, but they have recovered. Some, indeed, seem to have benefited by the separation.

Dr. Gardner mentions two suggestions which are often given to divorcing parents to which he takes exception. The first is that parents should be extremely careful to impress continually upon their children that the absent parent still loves them when he or she has walked out and continues to neglect the children. It is argued that it is important for the children to still feel loved by the parent who has left them. But what about the father, Gardner asks, who, living in the vicinity, hardly ever sees his children, or the father who abandons his family and is not heard from again for several years, if ever? What of the mother who runs off and forsakes her children? Do these parents love their children? Gardner does not think so. He insists that a child who is told that such a parent still loves them cannot believe it. The child may sense some duplicity and lose trust in the parent who tells him what he or she knows to be untrue. Some children are far better off when they are told that the absent parent has little, if any, love for them. This is *not* a reflection on the child. The child should be told that a parent's failure to love him or her does not make the child unlovable, nor does it mean that the child cannot be loved by someone else in the future. The child should be encouraged to seek love from those who can return it.

The second mistaken notion, Dr. Gardner believes, is that divorced parents should never criticize one another to the child. The rationale for this, he says, is that it is important to the child's healthy psychological development that he have respect and admiration for each of his parents. Only virtues are to be discussed. Here again, distrust and confusion can be created. The healthiest approach to such situations is to give the child an accurate picture of his parents as they really are: their assets and liabilities, their strengths and weaknesses. Like all humans, parents are not perfect. He should respect each in those areas that warrant respect, and hold in low opinion those qualities which are not worthy of admiration. This doesn't mean telling the child all the sordid details. Each parent has to be careful about an understandable lack of objectivity about someone they have divorced; still, when a father misses a visit and indicates a lack of interest in the child over a long period, it should be recognized for what it is. Likewise, when one parent denies him or herself a new suit so that the children can have the things they need, the other parent should praise this generous action for what it is.

Different factors appear to make a difference in outcome for children of different ages. For young children, the quality of parenting seems to be of primary importance. Young children seem to require that their mother—or custodial father—be both competent and caring; without being overwhelmed by the new demands on time and energy he or she must attend to their needs and be loving enough to make the child feel secure and worthwhile. Young children seem to do badly when the primary caretaker is enmeshed in continuing turmoil, or for other reasons preoccupied with his or her own life. They also do badly when the custodial parent runs them down.

For older children, not yet teenagers, brothers and sisters may be most helpful. The brother or sister can give them someone else to rely on, and someone else to share the burdens and opportunities of growing up in a single parent home. Supportive relationships outside the home in school activities, scouting, sports or church can be most helpful for these children. Maintaining close friendships is also very important for these children.

Most important for adolescents, especially older adolescents, seems to be the resilience and integrity already established in their developing characters. Those adolescents who were doing well at the time of their parents' separation seem much better able than others to cope with separation and more likely than others to return soon to their normal developmental progress. It seems important for children of all ages that their fathers continue to play a significant role in their lives.

The evidence now available does not warrant the conclusion that children whose parents divorce are more likely later in their lives to have emotional problems than children whose parents do not divorce. Certainly if there is an association between parental divorce and emotional disturbance, it is not a strong one. Yet we know from observation and from clinical studies that parental separation is severely upsetting to almost all children. How can this apparent inconsistency be explained?

First we should note that most children regain their developmental stride after parental separation despite their initial upset. Some, indeed, benefit. Among children who do not resume normal developmental progress, some were already having difficulty in school or elsewhere and simply continue to have difficulty after separation. For these children the separation did not make things worse. We might suspect that such troubled children are more likely to exist in families headed for separation than in other families, but perhaps the difference is not that great. Studies show that three-fourths of the children of divorce are not harmed by the experience. In the long run, this is only one of many critical incidents that shape these children, and in many cases there may be many other forces, especially a youngster's religion, which could counterbalance the shock of divorce. This is not to underestimate the fact that a small minority of children do sustain psychological damage at the time of parental divorce and these children need to be referred to competent counsellors.

Dr. Robert Weiss offers the following general principles that may help separating parents help their children:

1. *When parents separate, children, even very young children, should be kept informed about what is happening without overwhelming them with information they cannot assimilate.* Children will be less fearful if they are offered cogent explanations of what is happening, especially about those things which directly affect the shape of their lives. This can help prevent confusion in the child and the development of unrealistic threats. Such information can protect the children's self-esteem and relieve any fear that they caused the divorce.

2. *Children are likely to react to the divorce with upset and will need appropriate solicitude.* Younger children will need a lot of special attention to reassure them that life will continue fairly well for them; older children will need to have their negative feelings accepted and appropriate space offered for their personal recovery.

3. *Children who fail to resume normal development within a year of the separation may need special attention.* If the child is not again functioning in age-appropriate ways within the home, in school, and with friends, something may be going wrong. The parents together with the child should try to assess the situation, and if no modifications seem feasible, a professional child counsellor should be consulted.

4. *A competent and self-confident parent as head of the household is the child's most important source of security.* Children learn to rely on the custodial parent and learn how to cope with stress from this parent; the other parent should always support the custodial parent in every way possible for the good of the child.

5. *Pre-adolescent children need a parent's full attention at least part of the time.* The custodial parent may legitimately be absorbed in the tasks of reorganizing his or her own life, yet should be careful to set aside time every day to spend with the child. The custodial parent who feels hostile, punitive, and condemnatory toward his or her children should seek out a family therapist.

6. *Ordinarily, children gain if the non-custodial parent remains in the picture.* This parent can be a continuing source of security, love and support for the children of divorce.

7. *It is important for the children to retain as many regions of safety in their lives as possible.* It is important in the wake of a separation for children to remain in familiar, supportive settings of neighborhood, friends, school, church, and social activities. No unnecessary moves or adjustments should be placed upon the child at this delicate time.

8. *Insofar as there is change, children are likely to profit from parental support in establishing a satisfactory living situation for themselves.* Parents need to be involved in helping children relate to a new step-parent, adapt to a new school or church, make new friends, or become involved in new social activities. This will be hard on the children, but will be much easier if they feel they have their parents' support.

9. *Children should be permitted to mature at their own pace and neither be encouraged to become prematurely mature nor held back in their development through overprotection.*

10. *Parents can help their children by establishing satisfactory life situations for themselves.* Both the overly self-sacrificing parent and the overly protective parent can cause problems for children. The parent who concentrates on his or her personal recovery and establishes a new life after divorce, while not neglecting the children, will find in the long run that his or her recovery has helped the children.

Divorce adjustment counsellor Mel Krantzler, author of *Creative Divorce,* says that the plight of the divorced father is one aspect of the divorce crisis which has received little direct attention. "To many ex-wives, he is the 'lucky' partner, free from the daily responsibilities of child care, having only to send the monthly check and show up on time to pick up the children. To most of society, he is still the second parent—required to prove that he is a responsible father, but not expected to mind too much being separated from his children." Very often fathers experience an enormous sense of loss, the presence of unsuspected feelings of love and tenderness, and a wracking guilt. They are sometimes overwhelmed to discover how painfully they miss their children and the accustomed routines of past family life. While 93% of all divorce settlements presently award children to their mother, there is a growing awareness in the courts that many men are frequently more competent and sensitive parents than their former wives. "The best interest of the child" is now being interpreted to mean that fathers as well as mothers may have some form of joint custody of their children.

Custody arrangements of themselves cannot guarantee a close relationship between parents and children. Obviously it is the quality, not the quantity, of time spent together that counts. Some divorced fathers report that their relationships with their children actually improved after separation when they were forced to relate to their children in new ways and over more extended periods of time. Anything that can be done to structure better relationships and reinforce the relationships of the absent parent to the children of divorce is in the best interest of the children.

Rabbi Earl Grollman in his book, *Talking About Divorce,* says that some parents try to make up for their absence or compensate for their guilt by giving their children everything they want. Every trivial demand becomes a compelling command. A steady flow of expensive but unnecessary gifts pours in. The parents continue to spoil the child by doing only "fun things" and failing to discipline the child when necessary. They try to buy affection by being the "good guys." They do not advert to the fact that love cannot be purchased.

He advises parents not to try to make up by overindulgence. "A child needs to bend efforts toward achievement, but overindulgence deprives the youngster of attaining satisfactions by his own efforts." Further, he insists that the child should be given the privilege of growing up—occasionally being naughty and mischievous. Parents should be neither too demanding nor too permissive. "The goal is balance—something new easy for parents under any circumstances, especially divorced parents."

The rabbi offers some very wise concluding advice for the divorced parents:

You will get discouraged. At best, it is not easy to raise youngsters. Remember—everyone gets depressed during difficult periods of transition. Just as you don't demand too much from the youngster, so you should not create unrealistic requirements for yourself. Goals must be flexible. Take one day at a time. Accept what little you can do at the moment, even as you strive to accomplish a little more in the future. If you reject yourself as a failure, you will only create a more difficult environment for yourself and your child.

You can only bring alive an outlook that is authentic for you. The actual words you use are less important than the attitude you convey. It is only as you now search and find answers for yourself that you will help your child to search and find answers for himself or herself. This will demand your best wisdom, your most creative efforts. For the real challenge is not just how to explain divorce to your child but how to make peace with yourself.

References:

Gardner, Richard A. *The Boys and Girls Book About Divorce.* New York: Bantam Paperback, 1971.

Grollman, Earl A. *Talking About Divorce.* Boston: Beacon Press, 1975.

Krantzler, Mel. *Creative Divorce.* New York: New American Library, 1974.

Weiss, Robert S. *Marital Separation.* New York: Basic Books, 1975.

THE PARISH AND THE DIVORCED CATHOLIC

Being Catholic and divorced today is a poignant, painful, touching story. It's a story about people like Betty, Jack and Eleanor, members of Saint Christopher's, a Midwestern parish, all divorced, all now active in their local community and parish. It's the story of a caring pastor and his people and their struggle to help their divorced friends. It's fortunately a story that's being repeated today in every part of the country.

Saint Christopher's illustrates one of the most important facts about being a divorced Catholic today—divorce and remarriage no longer need separate people from the Catholic community. When Betty got divorced four years ago, she assumed that her divorce meant that she was no longer a Catholic. She stopped going to Church on Sunday. No one had told her she couldn't go, but she just felt she wasn't wanted—that she didn't belong. When she moved with her children to the city two years later, she was surprised to learn from a neighbor that the Catholic parish nearby had a support group for divorced people. She got up her courage and went to a meeting, and since then her life has changed dramatically.

Thousands of Catholics like Betty grew up believing that Catholics didn't divorce, and if they had to get a divorce, they were through as Catholics. Catholics learned in catechism class that Jesus was against divorce, and for that reason the Catholic Church did not permit divorce and remarriage. As true as that is, it could not justify the negative climate that came to exist in the American Catholic community toward divorced people, and could not explain the rejection and ostracism from family and Church that so many divorced people experienced. Betty says that when she was devastated by the breakup of her ten year marriage, she felt the need for her religion as never before, but felt abandoned by the Church. She felt closer to God than ever, and prayed daily, but there didn't seem to be anyone to turn to in the Church. She mentioned her situation in confession and was told coldly that she now had to learn to live alone, and if she ever got remarried she would be excommunicated from the Church. Instead of sympathy she received a harsh warning, and now feels that is why she drifted away from the Church.

Many American bishops and pastors became convinced in the early 1970's that the American Church law that attached a penalty of automatic excommunication from the Church to divorced Catholics who married again without the Church's approval, was one of the major causes of the negative, uncaring climate that so many divorced Catholics found in their local parishes. This was why the American Catholic bishops asked Pope Paul VI in 1977 to remove this law. The bishops had become convinced that this law, although originally intended 90 years before to prevent divorce, was really driving the divorced away from the Church at the very moment they needed the help of the Church community. Today when any one of the half million Catholics who will become divorced this year end their marriages, it is clear that their divorces do not separate them in any way from the Catholic community. The Church now recognizes that it has a Christian obligation to help those who suffer the heartbreak of broken marriage to find healing and new life.

When Betty became part of Saint Christopher's parish, she met a number of other divorced Catholics like herself through the parish support group. Betty immediately found that the friendship of other men and women who were coping with the same difficult adjustment problems was enormously helpful. Their meetings provided information on all kinds of important issues and a lot of informal sharing of some very practical advice about making it in today's society as a divorced person. For Betty as for every divorced person the breakup of her marriage was a profound spiritual crisis. At one evening's discussion she and about a dozen other divorced men and women shared some of the doubts and fears that had plagued them in the months after their separations. In addition to all the human dilemmas of going it alone in a couples society and managing all the practical demands of being a single parent, Betty and her new friends felt that divorce raised fundamental questions for them about the very meaning of their lives. They agonized over questions like: "Will I ever get over all this pain?" "Will I ever be able to love and trust anyone else again?" "Is God disappointed in me?" "Is God punishing me?" "What happened to the grace of the sacrament? This was never supposed to happen—how could God have let this happen?" "Will I ever be able to marry again and be accepted by the Church?"

Betty and the other members of the group were most fortunate that their pastor sat with them through their discussions and helped them shape a new Catholic identity. He helped them begin to think for themselves as Catholics, and he gave them valuable information about the Church's current approach to divorce and remarriage. This helped them move beyond the meager axioms of their childhood toward a more mature faith commitment. Most of all, he was a spiritual leader, who helped them pray, be reconciled to the sacraments, and move closer to a loving, understanding, accepting God.

With the help of the pastor, Jack had his failed marriage annulled. At first, Jack thought an annulment was out of the question for him because he and his former wife had three children. Father Bissett explained that children do not stand in the way of an annulment being granted nor are the children made illegitimate when a marriage is annulled. The failed marriage retains its civil legality protecting the children's civil rights, and further the Church guarantees that in no way will their place in the Church community be affected by the annulment of their parents' marriage. Jack at first told Father Bissett that he felt all the paperwork of the annulment was really unnecessary;

"Why doesn't the Catholic Church allow people to marry a second time like other Churches do? Wouldn't that be simpler?" Father Bissett explained that the Catholic Church has become convinced over its history that the best way to be faithful to the Lord's call to permanent marriage is not to bless second marriages. The Catholic Church maintains, he explained, that the family is the basic unit of society and strong, lasting marriages are essential to the well-being of the Church and society. All the recent Popes have worried aloud that so much divorce may weaken the very fabric of society. This doesn't mean that the Church is intransigent or unsympathetic to the divorced. It has over the past ten years streamlined the procedures for granting annulments, so that Catholics whose first marriages never had a chance of success can be freed from these marriages, and make a new marriage, if they choose, in the Church.

Father explained that the annulment process, as detailed and demanding as it is, is basically a monument to Catholic seriousness about permanent marriage. Furthermore it's a monument to Catholic respect for persons—the Church does not hold people to obligations they were unable to take on or keep. The tribunal is an instrument of the Church's compassion towards the divorced. With the help of Father Bissett, Jack had his first marriage annulled. Three years later he married a divorced woman who had also had her marriage annulled. Father Bissett officiated at that wedding, and said it was one of the most satisfying experiences of his priesthood.

Many other members of the parish support group have had their marriages annulled as well. Some say they cried tears of real joy when they finally got that piece of paper which said they were freed from all the lingering sorrow associated with their failed marriages. After her annulment was finalized, one group member told the group: "It really means a lot to know that the Church accepts the decision you made to divorce, and assures you that you did the right thing. I know now for sure that my marriage never had a chance."

Eleanor had been in her second marriage for fifteen years when she heard about Father Bissett. Her first marriage had lasted ten years before it ended in divorce. She had married a divorced Catholic in a civil ceremony, and their new marriage was full of the happiness that neither had found in their first marriages. Even though her new life was fulfilling in so many ways, Eleanor sorely missed the practice of her Catholic faith. Father Bissett met with Eleanor and her new husband, Bill. Over many meetings they became good friends. Since both previous marriages were invalid, Father tried everything possible to arrange annulments of their former marriages, but he could not assemble the necessary evidence.

As Father Bissett got to know Eleanor and Bill he began to see that they were generous, caring Christians; they were together raising the three children from Eleanor's first marriage as Catholics, and Bill was faithful in the financial support of the two children from his first marriage and saw to their religious upbringing. At Father Bissett's invitation they began to attend Sunday Mass, and became part of the support group for divorced Catholics. They proved to be most caring members of the group, several times offering their home to recently separated men who had nowhere to live. Bill, who is an accountant, volunteered to help on the parish finance committee. After several years and many conversations with Father Bissett, Eleanor and Bill began to receive Communion. Father Bissett explained to them that many pastoral authorities instruct the clergy to search out couples like Bill and Eleanor and try all available means of reconciling them to the sacramental life of the Church. Father Bissett exhausted all the public means of providing a blessing for their marriage through the annulment process, but that was not the end. After he became convinced that their first marriages were never true Christian marriages, and began to see that this new marriage had all the life signs of a solid, Christian union, he encouraged them to begin to receive Holy Communion. He explained that they should not see Communion as a blessing of their marriage or an approval of divorce and remarriage, but rather as a way in which the Lord reaches out to such couples through the Church community offering them the strength and healing of the Sacraments. Eleanor said that the Sunday she and Bill took Communion for the first time in 25 years was the happiest day of their lives.

The stories of Betty, Jack, and Eleanor and Bill, and Saint Christopher's, are being repeated in parishes all over the United States. A quiet, yet profound, revolution has begun to occur in the American Catholic Church. The Church community continues to take seriously the call of the Lord to permanence in Christian marriage and has redoubled its efforts to prepare the young better for marriage and provide better support for couples coping with the daily problems of contemporary marriage. The Church is learning that in no way does it compromise that service of lasting marriage by reaching out with compassion and support to those whose marriages have broken down. In fact, we are learning that we Catholics become much more attractive proponents of our traditional ideals when we are seen to be men and women who care for those who suffer from divorce. We are learning that there is a great deal the Church can do to help the divorced find healing and build new lives. The Church community can offer a sense of belonging and hope at this depressing time. The divorce crisis becomes for many men and women a time to thoroughly reorganize their lives. For many the simple verities of their childhood faith collapse under the complex strain of broken marriage, and they are forced to build a new adult faith commitment.

When Father Bissett and the other members of the pastoral team at Saint Christopher's became aware that there were so many divorced people in their parish, they discussed it at a weekly staff meeting, sharing their own impressions. It was suggested that they gather together a group of divorced persons from the parish and ask them how Saint Christopher's could help. Four divorced women and three men came to that first meeting at Betty's home. They told the priests that the main feeling they got from Saint Christopher's was that they didn't exist. They never heard a word about divorce from the pulpit or in the parish bulletin. They felt uneasy about knocking on the rectory door looking for help, for they were overly sensitive about being rejected again. There were problems with their children in the religious "ed" classes and embarrassment when they couldn't take Communion with their children. They knew of many more people in the area who had just given up on the Catholic Church because of divorce.

A month later the priests preached at all the Sunday Masses about the Church's concern for the divorced and remarried, explaining Jesus' special concern for the rejected and outcast. They wanted to find ways to reach out and help those who felt abandoned by the Catholic community. They called upon parishioners to contact their divorced Catholic neighbors and tell them that Saint Christopher's cared, and there was a place for them in the parish community. They then invited all parishioners who were interested, especially the divorced, to come to an open meeting at the parish the following Thursday evening.

About 75 people came to that meeting, which was chaired by the president of the parish council. There were many suggestions that emerged in the discussion that night: a support group for people going through marital separation and divorce; more sermons on Sunday about divorce among Catholics; some lectures in the parish adult education program on current thinking in the Church about divorce and remarriage; some special attention to the children of divorce; and some clear directive that divorced people were welcome to serve as lectors and CCD teachers and members of the parish council. A committee of divorced persons emerged from that meeting which became the steering committee of the new support group, and the parish council designated one of its members to work with the pastoral staff on making Saint Christopher's more sensitive to the needs of divorced persons.

The support group started out slowly but gradually the word spread and more and more people came, many from long distances because Saint Christopher's was the first parish in the area to do something for the divorced. The activities of the group were publicized in area newspapers and more and more divorced people began to surface. Two years later the coordinator of the Divorced Catholics Group became an *ex officio* member of the Parish Council, and a year later its president. Divorced people became visible in the life of the parish, bringing a special caring and a special vitality to its many programs. Men and women found recovery through the support group and moved onto other forms of service in the parish. The parish Director of Religious Education with the help of some divorced parents did consciousness-raising seminars for all the religion teachers so that they could better understand the special needs of children from single parent families. The parish First Communion program was adapted to more sensitively accommodate single parents.

Father Bissett says now that as divorced parishioners began to carry the burden of reaching out to others and taking responsibility for the parish's divorce ministry, his role became more specifically the special service only a priest can offer; he has become confessor, confidant, and healer helping many divorced become reconciled to the sacraments. He now tells other priests that the development of divorce ministry in the parish has been one of the most vital and significant renewal efforts of the life of the parish: "Saint Christopher's is known as the caring parish, and we're all very proud of that."

STARTING A PARISH DIVORCED CATHOLICS GROUP

1. Evaluating what the Parish is Already Doing for Divorced and Remarried

a. *Members of Pastoral Staff should discuss their individual approaches to separated or divorced persons.*

Discuss these questions: What kind of counseling and support is offered to those with severe marital problems? What kind of referrals are made? Are they effective? How do I look upon divorced persons? Do I consider them failures or rejects or incompetent persons? How have single parents been helped? When a divorced person approaches a member of the pastoral staff about remarriage, how is that handled? Might someone from the diocesan marriage tribunal be invited to a staff meeting to update members on local procedures, and how might staff assist in preparing cases? If there is no case for an annulment, and a couple is determined to marry, how is that handled? Are second married Catholics, whose marriages have not been blessed in the Church, ever reconciled to Communion? If so, how is this done? How is the public impact of such reconciliations explained? Has parish census or visitation given any indication of the number of separated, divorced and remarried persons in the parish? (In U.S. one in four Catholic adults has been divorced; one-third of our Catholic children live in single parent families or with remarried parents.)

b. *What messages does the parish presently send out about divorce and remarriage?*

Is it ever mentioned from the pulpit? If so, would divorced persons feel alienated by what is said? Has an attempt ever been made to preach on the Church's pastoral concern for those in broken marriages, and the responsibility of the Christian community to help those in difficult situations? Might not a Sunday be chosen for such a homily, such as Holy Family Sunday or the Lenten Sunday when the Gospel is about the divorced woman at Jacob's well? Are local helping resources for divorced persons ever mentioned in the bulletin? Is the subject of divorce and remarriage in the Church ever included in parish education programs or lecture series? What about the content of religious education programs for children and teenagers? Are negative stereotypes about divorced persons, branding them as bad Christians or failures, proposed in the classes? Has the religious education faculty met as a group to discuss content and the presence of the children of divorce in their classes? Are children told that divorce is a sin?

c. *Measuring what it is like to be divorced in this parish.*

First, gather together some divorced parishioners for feedback on their experience in this parish. (It might be best to hold such a discussion in a private home, so that they might feel freer to talk.) Ask how the parish might have helped when they were going through a divorce. Have they experienced any insensitivity or negative messages in preaching or classes? Has the parish been sensitive to the special needs of the children? How might the parish get further input about the needs of divorced persons in the area? Maybe an invitation in parish bulletin for feedback by mail or phone would be helpful.

d. *Consult with local resources about help available for the divorced.*
1. Diocesan family life office
2. Diocesan marriage tribunal
3. Other neighboring parishes, other Christian churches, and synagogues
4. Community mental health centers, counseling agencies, Catholic Charities
5. Schools and other welfare agencies

2. Getting a Group Started

a. *Announce at all the Masses* that this parish is concerned about helping people going through divorce and is trying to develop a parish program to help. The help of all parishioners is needed. Invite all parishioners to a parish meeting on topic such as "Where Are Divorced Catholics in the Church Today?" (Such a talk usually will attract the separated or recently divorced, some couples in second marriages, parents of divorced children, and parishioners who are intellectually curious about changes in the Church's life.) An opening presentation at this meeting (possibly given by an outside speaker) should be concrete and pastoral, not technical or canonical. Focus on ministry and reconciliation, and stress the Church's responsiblity to help. Those present will want to know about the status of divorced persons in the Church community, second marriages, reception of Communion, etc. There will be little awareness of how the Church might provide spiritual and emotional support at the time of divorce. (There will always be some people who have been hurt by poor pastoral care; be prepared for some anger.)

b. *At the end of the talk* and question period, invite all who would be interested in forming a parish support group to come back one week from tonight to discuss the shape of such a group. (Those who return usually will be the separated and divorced, those still struggling with many on-going problems. The remarried have solved their social needs; they usually need to see a priest or other pastoral minister privately about the status of their new marriage and receiving Communion.)

c. *At this first meeting,* have a few divorced persons designated as hosts, providing name tags and coffee. Make the atmosphere informal. Do not ask people to sign up on arriving since some may be anxious about coming and may be intimidated by joining up so soon; they may just want to sit and observe! Begin the meeting by asking how those present feel the parish could help, and offer them some concrete ideas of what a support group might be like. Invite them to share what it has been like being divorced and living in this parish. Be patient with the group; in time they will have plenty to say. Schedule another meeting, no more than two weeks away. (Groups need to meet at least every two weeks so that trust is not lost, and those who are hurting know there will be a meeting soon.)

d. *The convener of this first meeting* could be anyone on the pastoral staff or a member of the parish council or a divorced person. It is important that the pastor of the parish be present and show his support, even if he only drops by for a few minutes. The priest's role is as a back-up, serving as a symbolic ally, available for private consultation about religious questions.

3. What Goes on in a Support Group?

a. *When a marriage fails, a person's whole life often seems to crumble.* Depending on how painful the marriage was and how difficult the split, the divorced person is flooded with feelings of lowered self-worth, guilt, anxiety about the future, near-panic about raising children alone, and an acute sense of failure. It is a very isolating and lonely time, a time when one needs community and needs to belong. Since being married defines one's whole identity and social existence, when one divorces, one's social support system often collapses—the best friends and family members just don't seem to really understand how bad it is! One doesn't fit in any longer with married friends; relatives betray feelings of disapproval; one's standard of living is lowered and one's social life is curtailed. To be surrounded at this time by the company of other men and women who have been through the same bewildering transition, and made it, can be enormously helpful. These veterans can assure one that he or she will survive: "I know just how you feel!" "Here's what I did!" "Here's how I handled the kids!"

"This is how I consoled my broken-hearted mother!" "Here's how I handled loneliness, depression, and sexual anxiety!" Sharing and group formation in divorce groups is quick and strong.

b. *It is important not to communicate to divorced persons that they are sick and need treatment or therapy.* Most divorced persons go through a difficult transition (about one year for most) marked by passing symptoms of distress (anxiety, sleeplessness, loss of appetite, depression, euphoria, irritability, etc.), but most pull through it. A parish support group can help them get through it quicker and better, and may keep them from getting stuck. Have referral ready for occasional persons experiencing severe distress.

c. *Divorced persons need a lot of information* about their own emotional transition; raising children alone; their place in the Church, and what this failed marriage says about their relationship to God; prayer and putting together an adult faith commitment; taxes and financial matters; new friendships and dating; relating to family and former spouse. Regular presentations by knowledgeable helping professionals can be most important.

d. *The Rap Group:* Most groups provide "rap groups" for newcomers and those who have never really talked out their divorce experience. These groups are often facilitated by veteran divorced persons who have had some basic group leadership training. Such groups usually contract to meet for 6-8 weeks, and usually comprise 6-10 members. Ground rules are spelled out at the beginning guaranteeing confidentiality, no moral judgments, no "psyching" each other out, and no dating among group members.

e. *Home Masses, retreat days or evenings, weekend retreats, or special weekend models* such as The Beginning Experience (see below) can be most helpful in enabling people to develop the spiritual resources necessary to deal creatively with their on-going problems.

f. *Socials, wine and cheese parties, picnics, and sports outings* can be most helpful in filling the void left by the collapse of one's social network. Such gatherings can be especially helpful at holidays when memories of happier times can be most burdensome. These social activities might well include other parishioners; the divorced do not want to be isolated by themselves at all times.

g. *A group needs 50-100 members to survive.* There is a healthy turnover. Some people come for a time, and then don't come back. Others drop by from time to time whenever problems get tough. Others stay on in leadership roles, ministering to newcomers. Others stay on in quiet, helping roles. The group has to be big enough to provide for these various roles. Even the most caring persons have at best about a two-year life span in the group. This suggests that a parish support group might well serve a number of parishes in an area, with all the clergy supporting and feeding in members to the group.

h. *Structure of the Group:* Develop as much structure as is necessary to keep the group going. Don't re-found General Motors or re-write the Constitution of the United States. Most groups need a steering committee of 5-10 which handles on-going chores. Committee meetings should be open with everyone welcome who would like to help or chime in. Elect a chairperson every six months or so, so that strong persons don't dominate the group and weak persons don't destroy it. Designate someone from the group to be liaison with the pastoral staff and parish council to facilitate communication and support.

i. *Groups have proven most effective* in helping the recently separated and divorced over the divorce transition; many groups are now focusing on the special needs of the person who is recovered but now needs support in shaping an independent, single existence, especially single parents raising children alone or men living alone. Personal growth groups, retreat experiences, and opportunities for education and Christian service are especially important for these people.

4. Some Cautions

a. *Being divorced takes on different shape:* in urban or rural areas; predominantly Catholic or predominantly non-Catholic areas; among the young or the middle-aged; among the poor or financially more secure; among the educated or less well-educated. Every divorce group is different; be sensitive to what is appropriate in your area.

b. *It usually takes a good year for a group to be formed.* The group will struggle for a while. Usually word spreads by word of mouth. People are cautious at first and often suspicious. It will take time for lay leadership to emerge and feel confident.

c. *The goal of any group* is to reintegrate people into their parish, so there should be encouragement to move on and become part of other parish activities.

d. *Such a group is usually called a Divorced Catholics Group,* but not as a way of excluding those who are not Catholic. (Many groups have members who are not Catholic.) Rather there are some special problems and opportunities associated with being divorced and Catholic which gives this ministry a unique shape.

5. Resources

a. *Parishes with Good Divorced Catholics Groups*

1. St. Patrick's Church, Seattle, Wash. 98112 (Ms. Roni Bissett)
2. Holy Family Church, San Jose, Cal. 95123 (Ms. Hilary Nespole)
3. St. William's Church, Fridley, Minn. 55432 (Fr. Gil DeSutter)
4. St. Catherine of Siena Church, Riverside, Conn. 06878 (Ms. Betty Smith)
5. St. Margaret Mary Church, Winter Park, Fl. 32789 (Fr. John Bluett)
6. St. William's Church, Chicago, Ill. 60635 (Fr. Len Husk)
7. Our Lady, Star of the Sea Church, Marblehead, Mass. 01945 (Fr. Tom Ryan)
8. St. Columban's Church, Birmingham, Mich. 48102 (Fr. John Traecy)
9. St. Charles Church, Greece, N.Y. 14616 (Sr. Pat Norton)
10. Pope John XXIII University Parish, Knoxville, Tenn. 37902 (Fr. Charlie Brunick)
11. St. John the Apostle, Fort Worth, Tx. 76118 (Sr. Josephine Stewart)

b. The North American Conference of Separated and Divorced Catholics Sr. Paula Ripple, F.S.P.A., Executive Director, 5 Park St., Boston, Mass. 02108; (617) 367-1365. *(National clearinghouse for pastoral resources and models for divorced Catholics. Publishes* **Divorce,** *quarterly newsletter; sponsors annual conference at University of Notre Dame.)*

c. **"Catholics: Divorce and Remarriage"** Ten tape cassettes *(one hour each)* in which Father Jim Young interviews various experts and divorced Catholics themselves. Ideal for discussion groups. Write: NCR Cassettes, Box 281, Kansas City, Mo. 64141.

d. The Beginning Experience: weekend growth model for divorced persons; presented around U.S. for more information: Sr. Josephine Stewart, The Catholic Renewal Center of North Texas, 4503 Bridge St., Fort Worth, Tex. 76103; (817) 429-2920.

e. *Printed resources*

Grollman, Earl. **Explaining Divorce to Children.** Boston: Beacon Press, 1972. *A rabbi talks about the effect of divorce on children.*

Hunt, Morton and Bernice. **The Divorce Experience.** New York: McGraw-Hill, 1977. *A good overview of being divorced in America today.*

Krantzler, Mel. **Creative Divorce.** New York: New American Library, 1974. *A hopeful, helpful guide to making it through divorce.*

"*Ministering to the Separated and Divorced Catholic:* A Symposium," **The Living Light,** Winter, 1976. *A special issue of this religious education journal presents a readable overview of the Catholic discussion today about divorce and remarriage.*

Young, James J. C.S.P., editor, **Ministering to the Divorced Catholic.** New York: Paulist Press, 1978. *A collection of essays for pastors, ministers, concerned lay people and those involved in the Divorced Catholics Movement.*

PATHS OF LIFE

FAMILY HEALING PROGRAM

HEALING FAMILY HURTS—A book of readings and suggested actions on topics of concern to families. Areas treated include addictions, poverty, death, the handicapped, and physical abuse.

MINISTERING TO THE AGING—Information about the needs and gifts of older adults, including listings of resources for and about older persons.

GROWING THROUGH DIVORCE—A survey of information pertinent to the divorced Catholic and those who minister with them. Among the topics discussed are the effects of divorce on children, Jesus' teaching on divorce and remarriage, and how to start a parish divorced Catholics group.

FAMILY HEALING MANUAL—This resource for the parish staff includes programs, bibliographies and action suggestions on such topics as poverty, divorce, aging, death, and the handicapped.

AUDIO-VISUALS:

HEALING FAMILY HURTS—An examination of the various problems that families face and the effects of these problems on both the family unit and individual members.

GROWING THROUGH DIVORCE—Reflections on the experience of divorce, its effect on children, and the role the Christian community can play in ministering with the divorced and their families.